P. HARBISON

THE HIGH CROSSES OF IRELAND 2

RÖMISCH-GERMANISCHES ZENTRALMUSEUM

FORSCHUNGSINSTITUT FÜR VOR- UND FRÜHGESCHICHTE

MONOGRAPHIEN

BAND 17, 2

1992

DR. RUDOLF HABELT GMBH · BONN

RÖMISCH-GERMANISCHES ZENTRALMUSEUM
FORSCHUNGSINSTITUT FÜR VOR- UND FRÜHGESCHICHTE
IN VERBINDUNG MIT DER
ROYAL IRISH ACADEMY · DUBLIN

PETER HARBISON

THE HIGH CROSSES OF IRELAND

AN ICONOGRAPHICAL AND PHOTOGRAPHIC SURVEY

VOLUME 2: PHOTOGRAPHIC SURVEY

1992

DR. RUDOLF HABELT GMBH · BONN

Gedruckt mit Unterstützung des
Förderungs- und Beihilfefonds Wissenschaft
der VG WORT GmbH

Die Deutsche Bibliothek – CIP-Einheitsaufnahme

Harbison, Peter:
The high crosses of Ireland : an iconographical and
photographic survey / Peter Harbison. Römisch-Germanisches
Zentralmuseum, Forschungsinstitut für Vor- und
Frühgeschichte, in Verbindung mit der Royal Irish Academy,
Dublin. – Bonn : Habelt.
  (Monographien / Römisch-Germanisches Zentralmuseum,
  Forschungsinstitut für Vor- und Frühgeschichte ; Bd. 17)
  ISBN 3-7749-2536-4
NE: HST; Römisch-Germanisches Zentralmuseum <Mainz>:
  Monographien

Vol. 2. Photographic Survey. – 1992

Peter Harbison: The High Crosses of Ireland
Vol. 1: Text
Vol. 2: Photographic Survey
Vol. 3: Illustrations of Comparative Iconography

ISBN 3-7749-2536-4
ISSN 0171-1474

Figs. 1-2   Abbeyshrule, Co. Longford. Cross (Cat. 1): 1 East face. – 2 West face. – 2a South side.

Fig. 4 Addergoole, Co. Galway. Unfinished Cross-head. West face (Cat. **3**).

Fig. 3 Adamstown, Co. Wexford. »St. Abba's Cross«. South face (Cat. **2**).

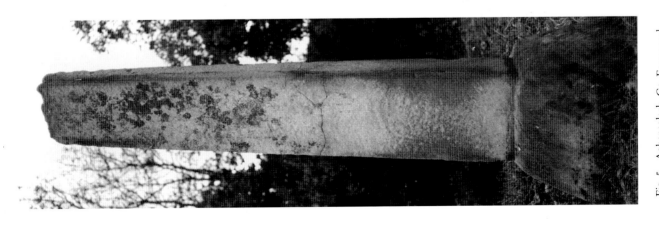

Figs. 6a-b   Aghowle, Co. Wicklow. Granite cross. West face (Cat. 5).

Fig. 5   Aghanaglack, Co. Fermanagh. Cross-shaft (Cat. 4).

Figs. 7-8   Ahenny, Co. Tipperary. North Cross (Cat. **6**): 7 East Face. – 8 Detail of shaft.

Fig. 9   Ahenny, Co. Tipperary. North Cross. East face. Detail of head (Cat. **6**).

Fig. 10 Ahenny, Co. Tipperary. North Cross. East face. Detail of base (Cat. **6**).

Fig. 11 Ahenny, Co. Tipperary. North Cross. South side. Detail of base (Cat. **6**).

Fig. 12   Ahenny, Co. Tipperary. North Cross. South side (Cat. 6).

Fig. 13   Ahenny, Co. Tipperary. North Cross. South side. Detail of shaft (Cat. **6**).

Fig. 14   Ahenny, Co. Tipperary. North Cross. West face (Cat. **6**).

Fig. 15   Ahenny, Co. Tipperary. North Cross. West face. Detail of upper part of shaft and head (Cat. **6**).

Fig. 16 Ahenny, Co. Tipperary. North Cross. West face. Detail of base and lower part of shaft (Cat. **6**).

Fig. 17   Ahenny, Co. Tipperary. North Cross. North side. Detail of base (Cat. 6).

Fig. 18   Ahenny, Co. Tipperary. North Cross. North side (Cat. **6**).

Fig. 19   Ahenny, Co. Tipperary. South Cross. East face (Cat. 7).

Fig. 20   Ahenny, Co. Tipperary. South Cross. East face. Detail of shaft (Cat. 7).

Fig. 21   Ahenny, Co. Tipperary. South Cross. East face. Detail of head (Cat. **7**).

Fig. 22   Ahenny, Co. Tipperary. South Cross. East face. Detail of base (Cat. 7).

Fig. 23   Ahenny, Co. Tipperary. South Cross. South side. Detail of base (Cat. 7).

Figs. 24-25   Ahenny, Co. Tipperary. South Cross (Cat. 7): 24 South side. – 25 Detail of shaft and under part of ring.

Figs. 26-27   Ahenny, Co. Tipperary. South Cross (Cat. **7**): 26 West face. – 27 North side.

Fig. 28 Ahenny, Co. Tipperary. South Cross. West face. Detail of base (Cat. 7).

Fig. 29 Ahenny, Co. Tipperary. South Cross. North side. Detail of base (Cat. 7).

Figs. 30-31 Arboe, Co. Tyrone (Cat. **8**): 30 East face of cross. – 31 Detail of shaft.

Fig. 32 Arboe, Co. Tyrone. East face of cross. Detail of head (Cat. **8**).

Figs. 33-35   Arboe, Co. Tyrone (Cat. **8**): 33 South side of cross. – 34 Detail of lower part of shaft. – 35 Detail of upper part of shaft and head.

Figs. 36-37 Arboe, Co. Tyrone (Cat. **8**): 36 West face of cross. – 37 Detail of shaft.

Fig. 38   Arboe, Co. Tyrone. West face of cross. Detail of head (Cat. **8**).

Figs. 39-41   Arboe, Co. Tyrone (Cat. 8): 39 North side of cross. – 40 Detail of shaft. – 41 Detail of head.

Fig. 42   Ardane, Co. Tipperary. Smaller cross-head. West face (Cat. **10**).

Figs. 43-44   Ardane, Co. Tipperary. Larger cross-head (Cat. **9**): 43 East face. – 44 West face.

Figs. 45-47 Armagh, Co. Armagh. Composite cross in Cathedral (Cat. **11/12**): 45 East face. – 46 South side. – 47 West face.

Figs. 48-49   Armagh, Co. Armagh. Composite cross in Cathedral. North side.   48 Detail of lower shaft fragment (Cat. **11**). – 49 Uppermost part of lower fragment, and part of upper fragment (Cat. **11/12**).

Figs. 50-51   Armagh, Co. Armagh. Head of cross in Cathedral (Cat. **11/12**): 50 East face. – 51 West face.

Fig. 54   Ballymore Eustace, Co. Kildare. South Cross. West face (Cat. 15).

Fig. 53   Ballinatray Lower, Co. Wexford. South face of cross as it was c. 1960 (Cat. 14).

Fig. 52   Armagh, Co. Armagh. Cross-fragment in Cathedral grounds. East face (Cat. 13).

Fig. 55   Ballymore Eustace, Co. Kildare. North Cross. West face (Cat. **16**).

Fig. 56   Ballymore Eustace, Co. Kildare. North Cross. East face (Cat. **16**).

Figs. 57-58   Ballynaguilkee Lower, Co. Waterford. Lost fragment of cross with decorated base (after Du Noyer watercolour in the Royal Irish Academy) (Cat. **17**).

N⁰ 3.c

Full size

Base of Cross at ancient burying ground .1 mile S of Ballynamult . C⁰ Waterford

N⁰ 4.c

Full size

Base of Cross at ancient burying ground Ballynamult C⁰ Waterford

Figs. 59-60   Ballynaguilkee Lower, Co. Waterford. Lost fragment of cross with decorated base (after Du Noyer watercolour in the Royal Irish Academy) (Cat. **17**).

Fig. 61   Ballynilard, Co. Tipperary. East face of cross (Cat. **18**).

Fig. 62   Ballynilard, Co. Tipperary. West face of cross (Cat. **18**).

Fig. 63   Balsitric, Co. Meath. Small cross-head in the National Museum (Cat. **19**).

Fig. 64 Balsitric, Co. Meath. Small cross-head in the National Museum (Cat. **19**).

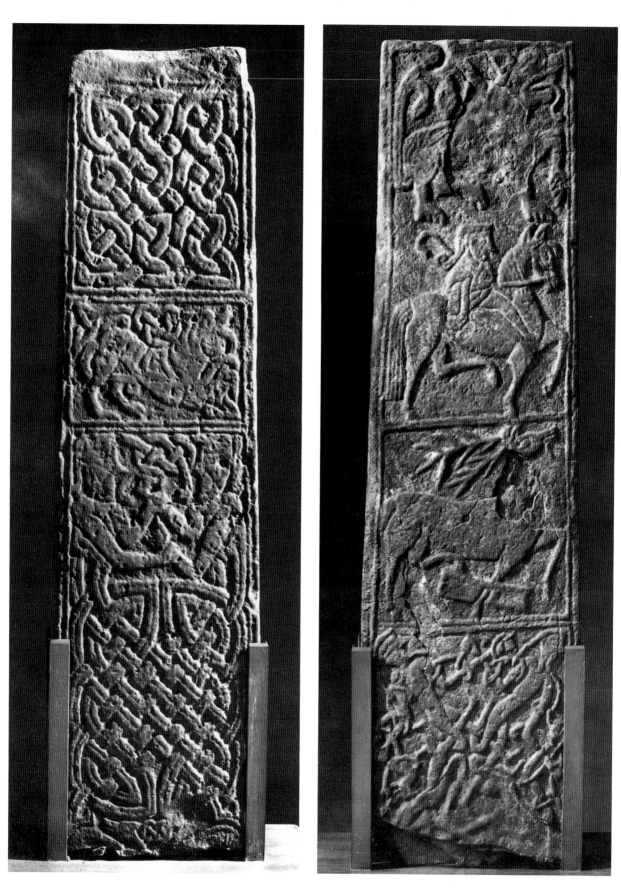

Figs. 65-66 Banagher, Co. Offaly. Shaft in the National Museum (Cat. 20): 65 Face 1. – 66 Face 2.

Figs. 67-68 Banagher, Co. Offaly. Shaft in the National Museum (Cat. **20**): 67 Side 1. – 68 Side 2.

Fig. 69 Bangor, Co. Down. Shaft-fragment in the chapel of Clandeboye House (Cat. **21**).

Figs. 70-71   Bealin, Co. Westmeath (Cat. **22**): 70 East face of cross. – 71 South side of cross.

Figs. 72-73   Bealin, Co. Westmeath (Cat. **22**): 72 West face of cross. – 73 North side of shaft.

Fig. 74 Blessington, Co. Wicklow. »St. Mark's Cross«, formerly at Burgage More (Cat. 23).

Fig. 75   Blessington, Co. Wicklow. A cross-head formerly at Burgage More (Cat. **24**).

Figs. 76-77   Boho, Co. Fermanagh. Cross-shaft (Cat. **25**): 76 East face. – 77 North side.

Figs. 78-79   Boho, Co. Fermanagh. Cross-shaft (Cat. **25**): 78 West face. – 79 South side.

Fig. 80 Boho, Co. Fermanagh. Fragment of cross-arm in the church porch (Cat. **25**).

Fig. 81 Broughanlea, Co. Antrim. North face of cross-head (Cat. **26**).

Fig. 82   Caledon, Co. Tyrone. Composite cross. West face (Cat. **27/28**).

Figs. 83-84 Camus, Co. Derry. Cross-shaft (Cat. **29**): 83 East face. – 84 South side.

Figs. 85-86 Camus, Co. Derry. Cross-shaft (Cat. **29**): 85 West face. – 86 North side.

Fig. 87   Carndonagh, Co. Donegal. West face of cross (Cat. **30**).

Figs. 88-89 Carndonagh, Co. Donegal (Cat. **30**): 88 East face of cross. – 89 South side of cross.

Fig. 90 Carrowmore, Co. Donegal. North
Cross (Cat. **31**).

Fig. 91 Carrowmore, Co. Donegal. South Cross. West face (Cat. **32**).

Fig. 92   Carrownaff, Co. Donegal. Cross (Cat. **33**).

Figs. 93-94   Cashel, Co. Tipperary. »St. Patrick's Cross« (Cat. **34**): 93 East face. – 94 South side.

Figs. 95-96   Cashel, Co. Tipperary. »St. Patrick's Cross« (Cat. **34**): 95 West face. – 96 North side.

Figs. 97-98 Castlebernard, Co. Offaly (Cat. **35**): 97 South face of cross. – 98 East side.

Figs. 99-100   Castlebernard, Co. Offaly (Cat. **35**): 99 North face of cross. – 100 West side.

Figs. 101-102   Castledermot, Co. Kildare. North Cross (Cat. **36**): 101 East face. – 102 South side.

Figs. 103-104   Castledermot, Co. Kildare. North Cross (Cat. **36**): 103 West face. – 104 North side.

Figs. 105-106   Castledermot, Co. Kildare. South Cross (Cat. **37**): 105 East face. – 106 North side.

Figs. 107-108   Castledermot, Co. Kildare. South Cross (Cat. **37**): 107 West face. – 108 South side.

Figs. 109-110 Castledermot, Co. Kildare. South Cross (Cat. **37**): 109 West face. Detail of shaft. – 110 Detail of head.

Fig. 111 Castledermot, Co. Kildare. South Cross. West face. Detail of base (Cat. 37).

Fig. 112   Castlekeeran, Co. Meath. North Cross (Cat. **38**).

Fig. 113   Castlekeeran, Co. Meath. South Cross (Cat. **39**).   Fig. 114   Castlekeeran, Co. Meath. West Cross (Cat. **40**).

Fig. 115 Clogher, Co. Tyrone. South and North composite crosses and cross-fragment between them. East faces (Cat. **41-45**).

Fig. 116 Clogher, Co. Tyrone. South Cross (with North Cross behind it). South side (Cat. **43/44**).

Fig. 117   Clogher, Co. Tyrone. South Cross. East face. Detail of head (Cat. **44**).

Fig. 118   Clogher, Co. Tyrone. North Cross. East face. Detail of upper half (Cat. **41/42**).

Fig. 120 Clogher, Co. Tyrone. South and North Crosses. North sides (Cat. 41-44).

Fig. 119 Clogher, Co. Tyrone. North and South Crosses. West faces (Cat. 41-44).

Figs. 121a-b   Clonca, Co. Donegal. East Cross (Cat. **46**): 121a East face. – 121b Detail of shaft.

Figs. 122 a-b   Clonca, Co. Donegal. East Cross (Cat. **46**): 122 a West face. – 122 b Detail of shaft.

Fig. 123   Clonca, Co. Donegal. West Cross (Cat. **47**).

Fig. 124   Clonca, Co. Donegal. West Cross. Fragment of arm in the church (Cat. **47**).

Fig. 125   Clonfad, Co. Westmeath. Shaft and head fragments (Cat. 50-51).

Figs. 126-127   Clones, Co. Monaghan. Composite Cross (Cat. **48/49**): 126 South-east face. – 127 South-west side.

Figs. 128-129   Clones, Co. Monaghan. Composite Cross (Cat. **48/49**): 128 North-west face. – 129 North-east side.

Fig. 130   Clonlea, Co. Down. North Cross. East face (Cat. **52**).

Fig. 131   Clonlea, Co. Down. South Cross. Base (Cat. **53**).

Fig. 132   Clonmacnois, Co. Offaly. Cross of the Scriptures. East face (Cat. **54**).

Figs. 133–134 Clonmacnois, Co. Offaly. Cross of the Scriptures. East face (Cat. **54**): 133 Detail of shaft. – 134 Detail of head.

Fig. 135 Clonmacnois, Co. Offaly. Cross of the Scriptures. East face. Detail of base (Cat. **54**).

Fig. 136 Clonmacnois, Co. Offaly. Cross of the Scriptures. South side. Detail of base (Cat. **54**).

Figs. 137-138   Clonmacnois, Co. Offaly. Cross of the Scriptures (Cat. **54**): 137 South side. – 138 Detail of shaft and underside of ring and arm.

Fig. 139   Clonmacnois, Co. Offaly. Cross of the Scriptures. West face (Cat. **54**).

Figs. 140-141   Clonmacnois, Co. Offaly. Cross of the Scriptures. West face (Cat. **54**): 140 Detail of shaft. – 141 Detail of head.

Figs. 142-143   Clonmacnois, Co. Offaly. Cross of the Scriptures (Cat. **54**): 142 North side. – 143 Detail of shaft.

Fig. 144 Clonmacnois, Co. Offaly. Cross of the Scriptures. West face. Detail of base (Cat. **54**).

Fig. 145 Clonmacnois, Co. Offaly. Cross of the Scriptures. North side. Detail of base (Cat. 54).

Fig. 146 Clonmacnois, Co. Offaly. Cross of the Scriptures. North side. Detail of the underside of ring and arm (Cat. **54**).

Figs. 147-149   Clonmacnois, Co. Offaly. North Cross (Cat. **55**): 147 South side. – 148 West face. – 149 North side.

Fig. 150   Clonmacnois, Co. Offaly. South Cross. East face (Cat. **56**).

Fig. 151 Clonmacnois, Co. Offaly. South Cross. East face. Detail of shaft (Cat. **56**).

Fig. 152   Clonmacnois, Co. Offaly. South Cross. East face. Detail of head (Cat. **56**).

Fig. 153   Clonmacnois, Co. Offaly. South Cross. East face. Detail of base (Cat. **56**).

Fig. 154   Clonmacnois, Co. Offaly. South Cross. South side. Detail of base (Cat. **56**).

Figs. 155-156   Clonmacnois, Co. Offaly. South Cross (Cat. **56**): 155 South side. – 156 West face.

Fig. 157   Clonmacnois, Co. Offaly. South Cross. West face. Detail of base and part of shaft (Cat. **56**).

Fig. 158   Clonmacnois, Co. Offaly. South Cross. West face. Detail of head (Cat. **56**).

Figs. 159-160   Clonmacnois, Co. Offaly. South Cross (Cat. **56**): 159 North side. – 160 Detail of shaft and underside of ring.

Figs. 161-162 Clonmacnois, Co. Offaly. Shaft fragment (Cat. **57**): 161 East side. – 162 North face.

Figs. 163-164 Clonmacnois, Co. Offaly. Shaft fragment (Cat. 57): 163 West side. – 164 South face.

Fig. 165 Clonmacnois, Co. Offaly. 'Pillar'. East side (Cat. **58**).

Figs. 166-167   Clonmacnois, Co. Offaly. 'Pillar' (Cat. **58**): 166 South face. – 167 West side.

Fig. 168   Clonmacnois, Co. Offaly. Fragment in the National Museum, Dublin. Main face (Cat. **59**).

Figs. 169-170   Clonmacnois, Co. Offaly. Fragment in the National Museum, Dublin (Cat. **59**): 169 Left side. – 170 Right side.

Fig. 171   Clonmore, Co. Carlow. North Cross (Cat. **60**).

Figs. 172-173 Clonmore, Co. Carlow. Cross-head (Cat. **61**): 172 East face. – 173 West face.

Fig. 174 Clontallagh, Co. Donegal. Undecorated cross (Cat. **62**).

Fig. 175   Cloonshanville, Co. Roscommon. North face of cross (Cat. **63**).

Figs. 176-177   Colp, Co. Meath (Cat. **64**): 176 East face of cross. – 177 West face of cross.

Figs. 179–180 Connor, Co. Antrim. Cross-fragment in the Rectory (Cat. **66**): 179 Face. – 180 Side.

Fig. 178 Cong, Co. Mayo. The sides and faces of a lost fragment of a 12th century cross (after Wilde) (Cat. **65**).

Fig. 181   Delgany, Co. Wicklow. Cross-shaft. South face (Cat. **67**).

Figs. 182-183 Donaghmore, Co. Down. Composite cross (Cat. **68/69**): 182 East face. – 183 Detail of shaft.

Fig. 184   Donaghmore, Co. Down. Composite cross. East face. Detail of head (Cat. **69**).

Fig. 185 Donaghmore, Co. Down. Composite cross. West face. Detail of head (Cat. **69**).

Figs. 186-188 Donaghmore, Co. Down. Composite cross (Cat. **68/69**): 186 South side. – 187 South side. Detail of shaft. – 188 North side.

Figs. 189-190   Donaghmore, Co. Down. Composite cross (Cat. **68/69**): 189 West face. – 190 Detail of shaft.

Figs. 191-192   Donaghmore, Co. Tyrone. Composite cross (Cat. **70/71**): 191 East face. – 192 Detail of shaft.

Fig. 193   Donaghmore, Co. Tyrone. Composite cross. East face. Detail of head (Cat. 71).

Figs. 194-195   Donaghmore, Co. Tyrone. Composite cross (Cat. **70/71**): 194 South side. – 195 Detail of lower part of shaft.

Figs. 196-197   Donaghmore, Co. Tyrone. Composite cross (Cat. **70/71**): 196 South side. Detail of underside of ring and arm. – 197 West face. Detail of shaft.

Fig. 198 Donaghmore, Co. Tyrone. Composite cross. West face. Detail of base (Cat. 70).

Figs. 199-200 Donaghmore, Co. Tyrone. Composite cross (Cat. 70/71): 199 West face. Detail of head. – 200 North side.

Figs. 201-202   Downpatrick, Co. Down. Cross outside the Cathedral (Cat. **72**): 201 East face. – 202 Detail of shaft.

Figs. 203-204   Downpatrick, Co. Down. Cross outside the Cathedral (Cat. **72**): 203 South side. – 204 West face.

Fig. 205   Downpatrick, Co. Down. North and South crosses in the south transept of the Cathedral (Cat. **73-74**).

Figs. 206-207 Downpatrick, Co. Down. Two fragments of a cross in the Cathedral porch (Cat. 75).

Fig. 210a   Dromiskin, Co. Louth. Cross-head. Underside of ring and north arm (Cat. 77).

Fig. 208   Downpatrick, Co. Down. Fragment of a cross (Cat. 76).

Figs. 209-210   Dromiskin, Co. Louth. Cross-head (Cat. **77**): 209 East face. – 210 West face.

Fig. 211 Dromore, Co. Down. Cross-fragments. East face (Cat. **78**).

Fig. 212   Dromore, Co. Down. Detail of the south side of the shaft-fragment (Cat. **78**).

Figs. 213-214   Drumcliff, Co. Sligo (Cat. **79/80**): 213 East face. – 214 West face.

Figs. 215-217 Drumcliff, Co. Sligo (Cat. **79/80**): 215 South side. – 216 South side. Detail of shaft. – 217 North side.

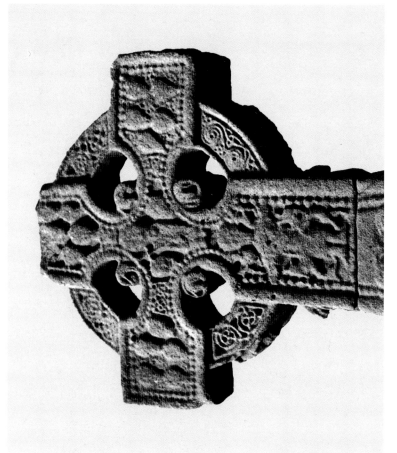

Fig. 219 Drumcliff, Co. Sligo. East face. Detail of head (Cat. 80).

Fig. 218 Drumcliff, Co. Sligo. East face. Detail of shaft (Cat. 79). The undecorated shaft, Cat. 82, can be seen in the left background.

Figs. 220-221 Drumcliff, Co. Sligo. West face (Cat. **79/80**): 220 Detail of shaft. – 221 Detail of head.

Figs. 222-223 Drumcliff, Co. Sligo. Lower cross-fragment in the National Museum (Cat. **81**): 222 East face. – 223 South side.

Figs. 224-225   Drumcliff, Co. Sligo. Lower cross-fragment in the National Museum (Cat. **81**):   224 West face. – 225 North side.

Figs. 226-227   Drumcliff, Co. Sligo. Upper cross-fragment in the National Museum (Cat. **81**): 226 East face. – 227 South side.

Figs. 228-229 Drumcliff, Co. Sligo. Upper cross-fragment in the National Museum (Cat. **81**): 228 West face. – 229 North side.

Fig. 231   Drumcullin, Co. Offaly. Cross-head. East face (Cat. **84**).

Figs. 230-230a   Drumcolumb, Co. Sligo. Cross-head (Cat. **83**).

Figs. 231a-232 Drumcullin, Co. Offaly. Cross-head (Cat. 84): 231a South side. – 232 West face.

Figs. 233-234   Drumgooland, Co. Down. Cross now at Castlewellan (Cat. **85**): 233 East face. – 234 South side. Detail of shaft and underside of ring and arm.

Figs. 235-236   Drumgooland, Co. Down. Cross now at Castlewellan (Cat. **85**): 235 West face. – 236 North side.

Figs. 237-238 Dulane, Co. Meath (Cat. **86**):
237 Cross-base. – 238 Cross-head arm-fragment, not now visible.

Figs. 239-240   Duleek, Co. Meath. North Cross (Cat. **87**): 239 East face. – 240 South side.

Figs. 241-242 Duleek, Co. Meath. North Cross. South side (Cat. **87**): 241 Detail of shaft. – 242 Detail of shaft and head.

Figs. 243-244   Duleek, Co. Meath. North Cross (Cat. **87**): 243 West face. – 244 North side.

Fig. 245   Duleek, Co. Meath. South Cross. East face (Cat. **88**).

Fig. 246   Duleek, Co Meath. South Cross. West face (Cat. **88**).

Fig. 247   Durrow, Co. Offaly. Cross. East face (Cat. **89**).

Fig. 248   Durrow, Co. Offaly. Cross. East face. Detail of head (Cat. **89**).

Figs. 249-250   Durrow, Co. Offaly. Cross (Cat. **89**): 249 East face. Detail of shaft. – 250 South side. Detail of shaft.

Figs. 251-252   Durrow, Co. Offaly. Cross (Cat. **89**): 251 South side. – 252 Detail of head.

Fig. 253   Durrow, Co. Offaly. Cross. South side. Detail of underside of ring (Cat. **89**).

Fig. 254   Durrow, Co. Offaly. Cross. West face (Cat. **89**).

Figs. 255-256   Durrow, Co. Offaly. Cross. West face (Cat. **89**): 255 Detail of shaft. – 256 Detail of head.

Figs. 257-258 Durrow, Co. Offaly. Cross (Cat. **89**): 257 North side. – 258 Detail of shaft.

Figs. 259-260   Durrow, Co. Offaly. Cross-head (Cat. 90): 259 East face. – 260 West face.

Figs. 261-262 Dysert O'Dea, Co. Clare (Cat. **91**): 261 East face. – 262 North side.

Fig. 263 Dysert O'Dea, Co. Clare. West face (Cat. **91**).

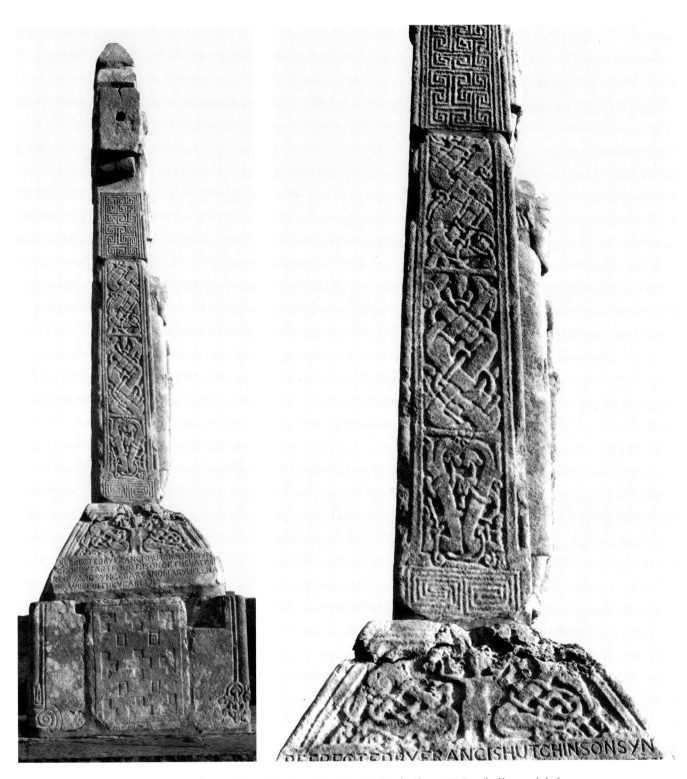

Figs. 264-265 Dysert O'Dea, Co. Clare (Cat. **91**): 264 South side. – 265 Detail of base and shaft.

Figs. 266–267 Eglish, Co. Armagh. East cross (Cat. **92**): 266 One face. – 267 The other face.

Fig. 268 Eglish, Co. Armagh. South cross (Cat. 93).

Fig. 269 Emlagh, Co. Roscommon. Cross-fragments, seen from the east (Cat. **94-97**).

Fig. 270   Emlagh, Co. Roscommon. Cross-fragments, seen from the south (Cat. **94-97**).

Fig. 271   Emlagh, Co. Roscommon. Cross-fragments, seen from the west (Cat. **94-97**).

Fig. 272   Emlagh, Co. Roscommon. Cross fragments, seen from the north (Cat. **94-97**).

Fig. 273   Emly, Co Tipperary. Imperforate cross (Cat. **98**).

Figs. 274-275   Errigal Keerogue, Co. Tyrone (Cat. **99**): 274 East face of cross. – 275 West face.

Fig. 276 Fahan Mura, Co. Donegal. Cross-decorated slab. East face (Cat.100).

Fig. 277 Fahan Mura, Co. Donegal. Cross-decorated slab. West face (Cat. 100).

Figs. 278-279 Ferns,
Co. Wexford. Shaft
(Cat. **101**): 278 East
face. – 279 South side.

Figs. 280-281 Ferns, Co. Wexford. Shaft
(Cat. 101): 280 West face. – 281 North
side.

Fig. 282 Ferns, Co. Wexford. West cross. West face (Cat. 102).

Fig. 283 Ferns, Co. Wexford. North cross. West face (Cat. 103).

Fig. 284   Ferns, Co. Wexford. North-east cross. West face (Cat. 104).

Figs. 285-286 Finglas, Co. Dublin (Cat. **105**): 285 East face of cross. – 286 South side. Underside of ring and arm.

Figs. 287-288   Finglas, Co. Dublin (Cat. **105**): 287 West face of cross. – 288 North side. Underside of ring and arm.

Fig. 289   Fore, Co. Westmeath. East face of cross (Cat. 106).

Fig. 290   Galloon, Co. Fermanagh. East cross. East face (Cat. 107).

Figs. 291-293   Galloon, Co. Fermanagh. East Cross (Cat. **107**): 291 South side. – 292 West face. – 293 North side.

Figs. 294-295   Galloon, Co. Fermanagh. West Cross (Cat. **108**): 294 East face. – 295 South side.

Figs. 296-297   Galloon, Co. Fermanagh. West Cross (Cat. **108**): 296 West face. – 297 North side.

Figs. 298-299 Galloon, Co. Fermanagh. Head-fragment (Cat. **109**): 298 East face, c. 1970. – 299 West face, c. 1966.

Figs. 300-301   Galloon, Co. Fermanagh. Lost head-fragment (Cat. 110):   300   East face, c. 1966. – 301   West face, c. 1966.

Fig. 303   Girley, Co. Meath. Lost cross-head (Cat. 112). – (After Du Noyer drawing in the Royal Society of Antiquaries of Ireland).

Fig. 302   Garryhundon, Co. Kilkenny. Cross (Cat. 111).

Fig. 304   Glendalough, Co. Wicklow. Market Cross. East face (Cat. **113**).

Figs. 305-306   Glendalough, Co. Wicklow. Market Cross (Cat. **113**): 305 South side. Detail of shaft. – 306 North side. Detail of shaft.

Fig. 307   Glendalough, Co. Wicklow. Market Cross. West face (Cat. **113**).

Fig. 308 Glendalough, Co. Wicklow. Cross near Reefert church. West face. Detail of head (Cat. **114**).

Fig. 309   Glendalough, Co. Wicklow. Cross near Reefert church. West face
(Cat. **114**).

Fig. 310   Glendalough, Co. Wicklow. Ringed cross
(Cat. **115**).

Figs. 311-312   Graiguenamanagh, Co. Kilkenny. North Cross (from Ballyogan) (Cat. **116**):   311 East face. – 312 South side.

Figs. 313-314   Graiguenamanagh, Co. Kilkenny. North Cross (from Ballyogan) (Cat. **116**): 313 West face. – 314 North side.

Fig. 315   Graiguenamanagh, Co. Kilkenny. South Cross (from Aghailta). East face (Cat. **117**).

Fig. 316 Graiguenamanagh, Co. Kilkenny. South Cross (from Aghailta). West face (Cat. **117**).

Fig. 317   Inishcealtra, Co. Clare. West Cross and East Cross ('Cross of Cathasach') (Cat **118-119**).

Fig. 318   Inishcealtra, Co. Clare. Ringed cross in St. Caimin's church. Head (Cat. **120**).

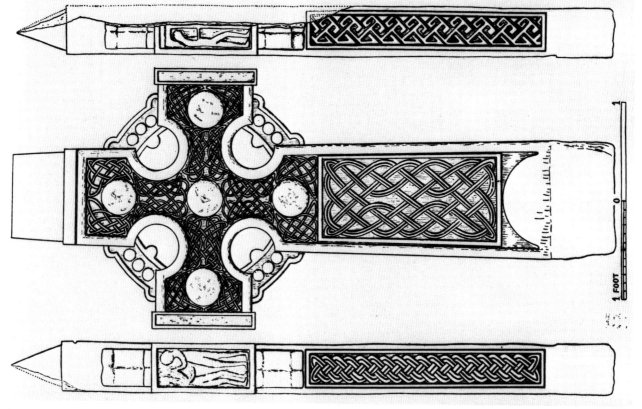

Figs. 319-320   Inishcealtra, Co. Clare (Cat. **120**):   319   Part of the head of the ringed cross in St. Caimin's church. Detail of end of arm. – 320   The ringed cross – after Macalister (1916b, Pl. XVIII).

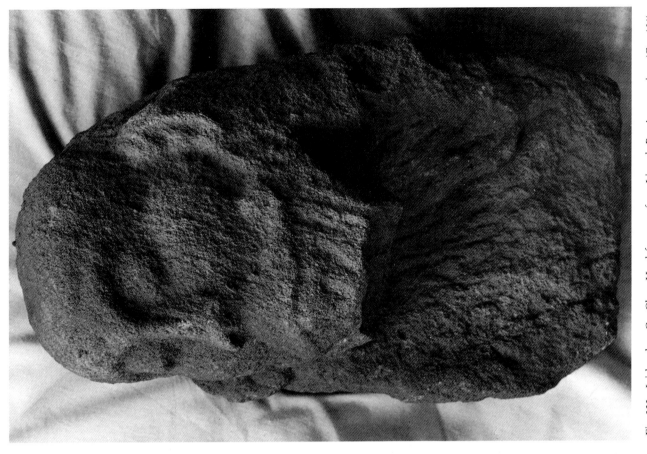

Fig. 322 Inishcealtra, Co. Clare. Head-fragment from Liam de Paor's excavations (Cat. **121**).

Fig. 321 Inishcealtra, Co. Clare. Part of the base and shaft of the ringed cross outside
St. Caimin's church. East face (Cat. **120**).

Fig. 323 Inishkeel, Co. Donegal. Cross-shaft. East face (Cat. **122**).

Fig. 324   Inishkeen, Co. Fermanagh. (?) Cross-shaft. East face
(Cat **123**).

Fig. 325   Inishmacsaint, Co. Fermanagh. Cross. East face
(Cat. **124**).

Figs. 326-327   Kells, Co. Meath. Broken Cross (Cat. **125**): 326 East face. – 327 South side.

Figs. 328-329   Kells, Co. Meath. Broken Cross (Cat. **125**): 328 West face. – 329 North side.

Figs. 330-331 Kells, Co. Meath. Market Cross
(Cat. 126): 330 East side. – 331 Detail of shaft.

Fig. 332 Kells, Co. Meath.
Market Cross. East side.
Detail of uppermost part of
shaft, and underside of ring
and arm (Cat. **126**).

Fig. 333 Kells, Co. Meath. Market Cross. East side. Detail of base (Cat. **126**).

Fig. 334 Kells, Co. Meath. Market Cross. South face. Detail of base (Cat. **126**).

Fig. 335   Kells, Co. Meath. Market Cross. South face (Cat. **126**).

Fig. 336   Kells, Co. Meath. Market Cross. South face. Detail of shaft (Cat. **126**).

Figs. 337-338   Kells, Co. Meath. Market Cross (Cat. **126**): 337 South face. Detail of head. – 338 West side. Detail of base.

Figs. 339-340   Kells, Co. Meath. Market Cross (Cat. **126**): 339 West side. – 340 Detail of shaft and head.

Fig. 341 Kells, Co. Meath. Market Cross. West side. Detail of underside of ring and arm. From a cast in the National Museum (Cat. **126**).

Fig. 342 Kells, Co. Meath. Market Cross. North face. Detail of base (Cat. **126**).

Fig. 343   Kells, Co. Meath. Market Cross. North face (Cat. **126**).

Fig. 344   Kells, Co. Meath. Market Cross. North face. Detail of shaft and head (Cat. **126**).

Fig. 345   Kells, Co. Meath. Cross of SS. Patrick and Columba. East face (Cat. **127**).

Figs. 346-347 Kells, Co. Meath. Cross of SS. Patrick and Columba. East face (Cat. **127**): 346 Detail of head. – 347 Detail of base.

Fig. 348   Kells, Co. Meath. Cross of SS. Patrick and Columba. East face. Detail of shaft (Cat. **127**).

Figs. 349-350   Kells, Co. Meath. Cross of SS. Patrick and Columba (Cat. **127**): 349 South side. – 350 Detail of shaft.

Figs. 351-352 Kells, Co. Meath. Cross of SS. Patrick and Columba. South side (Cat. **127**): 351 Detail of underside of arm. 352 Detail of head.

Figs. 353-354   Kells, Co. Meath. Cross of SS. Patrick and Columba (Cat. **127**): 353 West face. – 354 Detail of shaft.

Figs. 355-356   Kells, Co. Meath. Cross of SS. Patrick and Columba. West face (Cat. **127**):   355 Detail of head. – 356 Detail of base.

Fig. 357   Kells, Co. Meath. Cross of SS. Patrick and Columba. North side (Cat. **127**).

Fig. 358   Kells, Co. Meath. Cross of SS. Patrick and Columba. North side. Detail of shaft (Cat. **127**).

Fig. 359   Kells, Co. Meath. Cross of SS. Patrick and Columba. North side. Detail of underside of ring and of arm
(Cat. **127**).

Figs. 360–361 Kells, Co. Meath. Unfinished Cross. (Cat. **128**): 360 East face. – 361 West face.

Fig. 363   Kells, Co. Meath. Decorated cross-base (Cat. **129**).

Fig. 362   Kells, Co. Meath. Unfinished Cross. South side. Underside of ring and arm (Cat. **128**).

Fig. 364   Kilbroney, Co. Down. West face of cross (Cat. **130**).

Fig. 366 Kilcoo, Co. Fermanagh. Base and shaft of a cross (Cat. 132).

Fig. 365 Kilcashel, Co. Donegal. »St. Conall's Cross« (Cat. 131).

Figs. 367-368   Kilfenora, Co. Clare. »Doorty Cross« (Cat. **133**): 367 East face. – 368 South side.

Figs. 369-370   Kilfenora, Co. Clare. »Doorty Cross« (Cat. **133**): 369 West face. – 370 North side.

Figs. 371-372   Kilfenora, Co. Clare. North Cross (Cat. **134**): 371 East face. – 372 West face.

Figs. 373-374   Kilfenora, Co. Clare. South Cross (Cat. **135**): 373 East face. – 374 West face.

Figs. 375-376   Kilfenora, Co. Clare. West Cross (Cat. **136**): 375 East face. – 376 West face.

Fig. 377 Kilfenora, Co. Clare. West Cross. West Face. Detail of head (Cat. **136**).

Figs. 378-379 Kilfenora, Co. Clare. Shaft-fragment in the Cathedral chancel (Cat. 137): 378 East face. – 379 West face.

Fig. 380 Kilfenora, Co. Clare. Shaft-fragment (Cat. 138).

Fig. 381   Kilgobbin, Co. Dublin. East face of cross (Cat. **139**).

Fig. 382   Kilgobbin, Co. Dublin. Head of west face of cross (Cat. **139**).

Fig. 383   Kilkieran, Co. Kilkenny. East Cross. East face (Cat. 140).

Figs. 384-385   Kilkieran, Co. Kilkenny. East Cross (Cat. **140**): 384 East face. Detail of head. – 385 West face. Detail of Head.

Fig. 386   Kilkieran, Co. Kilkenny. South Cross. East face (Cat. **141**).

Fig. 387   Kilkieran, Co. Kilkenny. West Cross. East face. Shaft and head (Cat. **142**).

Fig. 388 Kilkieran, Co. Kilkenny. West Cross. East face. Base. Southern half (Cat. 142).

Fig. 389   Kilkieran, Co. Kilkenny. West Cross. East face. Base. Northern half (Cat. **142**).

Figs. 390-391   Kilkieran, Co. Kilkenny. West Cross (Cat. **142**): 390 South side. – 391 West face.

Figs. 392-393   Kilkieran, Co. Kilkenny. West Cross (Cat. **142**): 392 West face. – 393 North side.

Fig. 394 Kilkieran, Co. Kilkenny. Cross-fragment. Face 1 (Cat. **143**).

Fig. 395   Kilkieran, Co. Kilkenny. Cross-fragment. Face 2 (Cat. **143**).

Figs. 396-397 Kilkieran, Co. Kilkenny. Cross-fragments (Cat. **143**): 396 Face 1. – 397 Face 2.

KILKIERAN HIGH CROSS

CONJECTURAL RESTORATION   SCALE   DRAWN BY R.W. STAPLETON

0   50   100 cms

Fig. 398   Kilkieran, Co. Kilkenny. Fragmentary Cross (Cat. **143**) (Reconstruction by R. W. Stapleton).
Face 1 is on the left, Face 2 on the right.

Figs. 398 a-b   Kilkieran, Co. Kilkenny. Cross-fragments. Face 1 (Cat. **143**).

Figs. 398 c-d   Kilkieran, Co. Kilkenny. Cross-fragments. Face 2 (Cat. **143**).

Fig. 399   Killaloe, Co. Clare. Cross from Kilfenora. East face (Cat. **144**).

Fig. 400 Killaloe, Co. Clare. Cross from Kilfenora. Face now attached to wall, as seen around 1930 (Cat. 144).

Fig. 401 Killaloe, Co. Clare. Fragmentary shaft. East side, with Ogham inscription (Cat. 145).

Fig. 402   Killaloe, Co. Clare. Fragmentary shaft. South face (Cat. **145**).

Fig. 403　Killaloe, Co. Clare. Fragmentary shaft. North face, with Runic inscription (Cat. **145**).

Fig. 404   Killamery, Co. Kilkenny. East face of cross (Cat. **146**).

Fig. 405   Killamery, Co. Kilkenny. East face of cross. Detail of head (Cat. **146**).

Figs. 406-407   Killamery, Co. Kilkenny (Cat. **146**): 406 South side of cross. – 407 Detail of head.

Fig. 408   Killamery, Co. Kilkenny. North side of cross (Cat. **146**).

Fig. 409 Killamery, Co. Kilkenny. East face of cross. Detail of base (Cat. 146).

Fig. 410 Killamery, Co. Kilkenny. West face of cross. Detail of base (Cat. **146**).

Fig. 411   Killamery, Co. Kilkenny. West face of cross (Cat. **146**).

Fig. 412   Killamery, Co. Kilkenny. West face of cross. Detail of head (Cat. **146**).

Figs. 413-414   Killary, Co. Meath. Cross-shaft (Cat. **147**): 413 South side. – 414 East face.

Figs. 415-416   Killary, Co. Meath. Cross-shaft (Cat. **147**): 415 West face. – 416 North side.

a

b

c

Figs. 417a-c Killary, Co. Meath (Cat. **148-148a**): 417a-b Fragments of cross-shaft. – 417c Cross-head fragment, with base.

Figs. 418-419   Killeany/Teaglach Éinne, Co. Galway. Shaft fragment at Killeany (Cat. **149 a**):   418 South side. – 419 North side.

Fig. 420   Killeany/Teaglach Éinne, Co. Galway. Shaft fragment at Killeany. East face (Cat. **149 a**).

Fig. 421   Killeany/Teaglach Éinne, Co. Galway. Shaft fragment at Killeany. West face (Cat. **149 a**).

Fig. 422   Killeany/Teaglach Éinne, Co. Galway. Shaft fragments at Teaglach Éinne. North face (Cat. **149 b**).

Figs. 423-426 Killeany/Teaglach Éinne, Co. Galway. 423 Reconstruction of fragments at Killeany (Cat. **149a**) and Teaglach Éinne (Cat. **149b**). The position of b ist doubtful (after Henry 1970). – 424-426 Shaft fragments at Teaglach Éinne. South face (Cat. **149b**): 424 Original top of head, now inserted upside down on the bottom; 425 Top fragment; 426 Present middle fragment.

Figs. 427 a-b   Killeany/Teaglach Éinne, Co. Galway. Cross-head from Teaglach Éinne (Cat. **150**):
427 a Face 1. – 427 b Face 2.

Fig. 428   Killegar, Co. Wicklow. Fragment of cross-head (Cat. **151**).

Fig. 429   Killinaboy, Co. Clare. Tau Cross (Cat. **153**).

Fig. 430 Killesher, Co. Fermanagh. Cross-head in the County Museum, Enniskillen. Face 2 (Cat. **152**).

Fig. 431   Killesher, Co. Fermanagh. Cross-head in the County Museum, Enniskillen. Face 1 (Cat. **152**).

Fig. 432   Killoan, Co. Tyrone. Decorated base.South face (Cat. **155**).

Fig. 433   Killiney, Co. Kerry. West face of cross (Cat. **154**).

Fig. 434   Kill of the Grange, Co. Dublin. Cross (Cat. **156**).

Figs. 435-436 Kilmainham, Co. Dublin. Cross-shaft (Cat. **157**): 435 East face. – 436 West face.

Fig. 437   Kilmalkedar, Co. Kerry. West face of cross (Cat. **158**).

Figs. 438-439   Kilmokea, Co. Wexford (Cat. **159**): 438 East face of cross. – 439 South side.

Fig. 440   Kilmokea, Co. Wexford. West face of cross (Cat. **159**).

Figs. 441-442 Kilnaruane, Co. Cork. Cross-shaft (Cat. 160): 441 West face. – 442 Upper part of east face.

Fig. 443 Kilquiggin, Co. Wicklow. Cross-head (Cat. **161**).

Figs. 444-445 Kilree, Co. Kilkenny (Cat. **162**): 444 South side of cross. – 445 North side.

Fig. 446   Kilree, Co. Kilkenny. East face of cross (Cat. **162**).

Fig. 447   Kilree, Co. Kilkenny. West face of cross (Cat. **162**).

Figs. 448-449   Kilteel, Co. Kildare. Cross-head and base (Cat. **163**): 448 East face. – 449 West face.

Figs. 450-451 Knock, Co. Meath (Cat. **164**): 450 East face of cross. – 451 West face.

Figs. 452-453 Leggettsrath, Co. Kilkenny. Fragments of cross-shaft and head (Cat. **165**): 452 East face. – 453 West face.

Fig. 454 Lismore,   Co.   Waterford.
Cross-head in the Cathedral (Cat. **166**).

Figs. 455–456   Lisnaskea, Co. Fermanagh. Cross-shaft (Cat. **167**):   455   North-east face. – 456   South-west face.

Figs. 457-458 Lorrha, Co. Tipperary. North-west Cross (Cat. **168**): 457 East face. – 458 South side.

Figs. 459–460 Lorrha, Co. Tipperary. North-west Cross (Cat. **168**): 459 West face. – 460 North side.

Fig. 461 Lorrha, Co. Tipperary. South-east Cross. West face (Cat. **169**).

Fig. 462   Lorrha, Co. Tipperary. South-east Cross. North side (Cat. **169**).

Fig. 463   Lorrha, Co. Tipperary. South-east Cross. East face. Shaft (Cat. **169**).

Fig. 464   Lorum, Co. Carlow. Shaft-fragment. West face (Cat. **170**).

Fig. 465   Magharees, Co. Kerry. West face of cross (Cat. 171).

Figs. 466-467   Monaincha, Co. Tipperary. Cross-head (Cat. **172**): 466 East face. – 467 South side.

Figs. 468-469 Monaincha, Co. Tipperary. Cross-head (Cat. **172**): 468 West face. – 469 North side.

Fig. 470   Monaincha, Co. Tipperary. Cross-base. South side (Cat. **172**).

Fig. 471   Monaincha, Co. Tipperary. Head-fragment (Cat. **173**).

Fig. 472   Monasterboice, Co. Louth. Muiredach's Cross. East face (Cat. **174**).

Fig. 473   Monasterboice, Co. Louth. Muiredach's Cross. East face. Detail of shaft and head (Cat. **174**).

Figs. 474-475   Monasterboice, Co. Louth. Muiredach's Cross (Cat. **174**): 474 South side. – 475 Detail of head.

Fig. 476   Monasterboice, Co. Louth. Muiredach's Cross. South side. Detail of shaft (Cat. **174**).

Fig. 477   Monasterboice, Co. Louth. Muiredach's Cross. South side. Detail of underside of ring and arm (Cat. **174**).

Fig. 478   Monasterboice, Co. Louth. Muiredach's Cross. East face. Detail of base (Cat. 174).

Fig. 479   Monasterboice, Co. Louth. Muiredach's Cross. South side. Detail of base (Cat. 174).

Fig. 480   Monasterboice, Co. Louth. Muiredach's Cross. West face (Cat. 174).

Fig. 481   Monasterboice, Co. Louth. Muiredach's Cross. West face. Detail of upper part of shaft and head (Cat. **174**).

Fig. 482   Monasterboice, Co. Louth. Muiredach's Cross. West face. Detail of base and lower part of shaft (Cat. **174**).

Fig. 483   Monasterboice, Co. Louth. Muiredach's Cross. North side. Detail of base (Cat. **174**).

Figs. 484-486 Monasterboice, Co. Louth. Muiredach's Cross (Cat. **174**): 484 North side. – 485 Detail of head. – 486 Detail of shaft.

Fig. 487   Monasterboice, Co. Louth. Muiredach's Cross. North side. Detail of underside of ring and arm (Cat. **174**).

Figs. 488-489   Monasterboice, Co. Louth. Tall Cross (Cat. **175**): 488   East face. – 489   Detail of shaft.

Fig. 490 Monasterboice, Co. Louth. Tall Cross. East face. Detail of head (Cat. **175**).

Figs. 491-492　Monasterboice, Co. Louth. Tall Cross (Cat. **175**): 491　South side. – 492　Detail of shaft.

Fig. 493   Monasterboice, Co. Louth. Tall Cross. South side. Detail of top of shaft and underside of ring
(Cat. **175**).

Figs. 494-495   Monasterboice, Co. Louth. Tall Cross (Cat. **175**): 494   West face. – 495   Detail of shaft.

Fig. 496   Monasterboice, Co. Louth. Tall Cross. West Face. Detail of head (Cat. **175**).

Figs. 497-498 Monasterboice, Co. Louth. Tall Cross. North side (Cat. **175**): 497 Part of shaft. – 498 Detail of upper part of shaft and head.

Fig. 499 Monasterboice, Co. Louth. Tall Cross. North side. Detail of top of shaft and underside of ring (Cat. **175**).

Figs. 500-501 Monasterboice, Co. Louth. North Cross (Cat. **177**): 500 East face. – 501 West face.

Fig. 503 Monasterboice, Co. Louth. Cross-shaft. South side (Cat. 178).

Fig. 502 Monasterboice, Co. Louth. North Cross. Fragment of the bottom of a shaft. South face (Cat. 176).

Figs. 504-505 Monaster-
boice, Co. Louth. Head-fragment in the National Museum
(Cat. **179**): 504 Face 1. – 505
Face 2.

Fig. 506   Monasterboice, Co. Louth. Head-fragment in the National Museum.
End of arm (Cat. **179**).

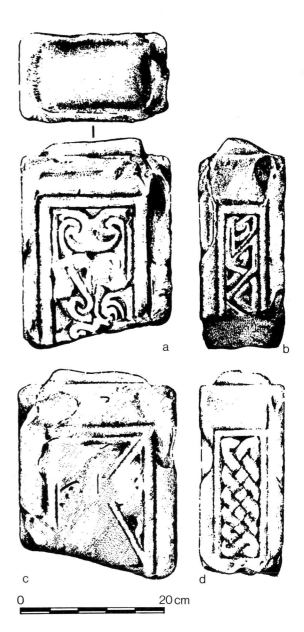

a

b

c

d

0   20 cm

Fig. 507   Monasterboice, Co. Louth. Shaft-fragment in the
National Museum (Cat. **180**).

Figs. 508-509   Moone, Co. Kildare. Cross (Cat. **181**): 508 East face. – 509 Detail of base.

Figs. 510-511   Moone, Co. Kildare. Cross. East face (Cat. **181**): 510 Detail of shaft. – 511 Detail of head.

Figs. 512-513   Moone, Co. Kildare. Cross (Cat. **181**): 512 South side. – 513 Detail of base.

Figs. 514-515   Moone, Co. Kildare. Cross (Cat. **181**): 514 West face. – 515 Detail of base.

Figs. 516-517   Moone, Co. Kildare. Cross (Cat. **181**): 516 West face. Detail of shaft and head. – 517 North side.

Figs. 518-519   Moone, Co. Kildare. Cross. North side (Cat. **181**): 518 Detail of base. – 519 Detail of shaft.

Figs. 520b.521b Moone, Co. Kildare. Fragmentary cross. Upper shaft and head fragments (Cat. **182**): 520b East face. – 521b West face.

Figs. 520a.521a   Moone, Co. Kildare. Fragmentary cross. Lower shaft fragment (Cat. **182**): 520a   East face. – 521a   West face.

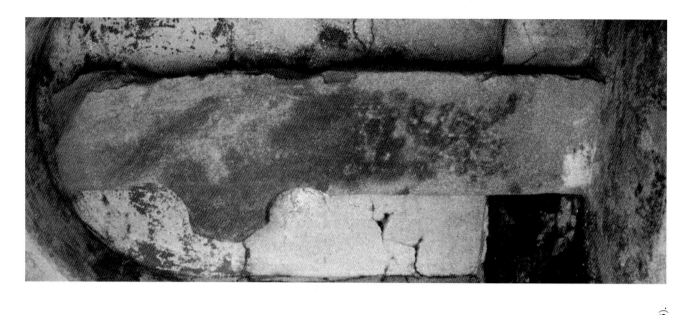

Fig. 522   Moone, Co. Kildare. Fragmentary cross. Drawing of the faces and sides of the lowest part of the shaft – after O'Neill 1857
Pl. XVIII (Cat. 182).

Fig. 523   Mullaboy, Co. Derry (Cat. 183).

Figs. 524-525 Newtown,
Co. Carlow. Cross-head
(Cat. **184**): 524 East face. –
525 West face.

Fig. 526 Noughaval, Co. Clare. West face of cross (Cat. **185**).

Fig. 527   Nurney, Co. Carlow. South face of cross (Cat. **186**).

Figs. 528-529 Oldcourt, Co. Wicklow. Base (Cat. 187): 528 East face. – 529 South face.

Fig. 531   Old Kilcullen, Co. Kildare. East shaft. South face (Cat. 188).

Fig. 530   Oldcourt, Co. Wicklow. Base. West face (Cat. 187).

Figs. 532-533   Old Kilcullen, Co. Kildare. West shaft (Cat. **189**): 532 East face. – 533 South side.

Figs. 534-535   Old Kilcullen, Co. Kildare. West shaft (Cat. **189**): 534 West face. – 535 North side.

Fig. 536   Old Leighlin, Co. Carlow. Cross (Cat. **190**).

Figs. 537-538 Orchard,
Co. Carlow (Cat. **191**):
537 Base. – 538 Cross-
fragment.

Fig. 539   Ray, Co. Donegal. South face of cross (Cat. **192**).

Fig. 540   Reenconnell, Co. Kerry. East face of cross (Cat. **193**).

Figs. 541-542   Roscrea, Co. Tipperary. Cross. Lower fragment (Cat. **194**): 541 East face. – 542 South side.

Figs. 543-544 Roscrea, Co. Tipperary (Cat. **194**): 543 Lower and upper fragment. West face. – 544 Lower fragment. North side.

Fig. 545 Roscrea, Co. Tipperary. Upper fragment. East face (Cat. 194).

Figs.546-547 Roscrea, Co. Tipperary. Upper fragment (Cat. **194**): 546 South side. – 547 North side. Top of shaft and underside of arm.

Fig. 548   Roscrea, Co. Tipperary. Pillar. East face (Cat. **195**).

Figs. 549-550   Roscrea, Co. Tipperary. Pillar (Cat. **195**): 549 South side. – 550 North side.

Figs. 551-553   St. Macdara's Island, Co. Galway. Cross-fragments (Cat. **196/197**).

Fig. 554 St. Mullins, Co. Carlow. East face of cross (Cat. **198**).

Figs. 555-556 St. Mullins, Co. Carlow (Cat. **198**): 555 West face of cross. – 556 East face. Detail of base.

Figs. 557-558   St. Mullins, Co. Carlow (Cat. **198**): 557 South side of cross. – 558 North side.

Fig. 559 Seir Kieran, Co. Offaly. Base. East face (Cat. 199).

Fig. 560   Seir Kieran, Co. Offaly. Base. South face (Cat. 199).

Fig. 561   Seir Kieran, Co. Offaly. Base. North face (Cat. 199).

Fig. 563   Selloo, Co. Monaghan. Portion (probably the shaft) of a cross. (Now in the County Museum in Monaghan) (Cat. 201).

Fig. 562   Seir Kieran, Co. Offaly. Cross (Cat. 200).

Fig. 565 Sleaty, Co. Laois. South Cross. West face (Cat. 204).

Fig. 564 Sleaty, Co. Laois. North Cross. West face (Cat. 203).

Fig. 567 Taghmon, Co. Wexford. Base and Cross-head. South face (Cat. **205**).

Fig. 566 Skeaghavannoe, Co. Clare. Cross-head (Cat. **202**).

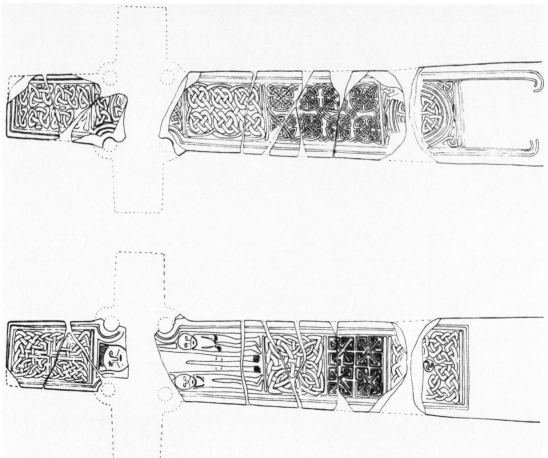

Figs. 568-569 Temple Brecan, Inishmore, Co. Galway. North Cross (Cat. **206**): 568 Reconstruction of the east (left) and west (right) faces (after Waddell 1981). 569 East face. Bottom fragment of shaft (standing).

Figs. 570-571   Temple Brecan, Inishmore, Co. Galway. North Cross. East face (Cat. **206**): 570 Fragment of shaft. – 571 Fragments of shaft and head.

Fig. 572 Temple Brecan, Inishmore, Co. Galway. North Cross. East face. Fragments of head (Cat. **206**).

Figs. 573-574   Temple Brecan, Inishmore, Co. Galway. North Cross. West face (Cat. **206**): 573 Bottom fragment of shaft. – 574 Fragments of shaft and head.

Figs. 575-576   Temple Brecan, Inishmore, Co. Galway (Cat. **207**): 575 South Cross. – 576 Drawing of the South Cross (after Westropp).

Figs. 577-578   Temple Brecan, Inishmore, Co. Galway. West Cross (Cat. **208**): 577 East face. Shaft. – 578 West face. Shaft.

Fig. 579   Temple Brecan, Inishmore, Co. Galway. West Cross. Reconstruction of the east (left) and west (right) faces kindly
supplied by Dr. John Waddell, University College, Galway (Cat. 208).

Figs. 580-581   Temple Brecan, Inishmore, Co. Galway. West Cross (Cat. **208**): 580 East face. Head-fragments. – 581 West
face. Head-fragments.

Fig. 582   Termonfechin, Co. Louth. East face of cross (Cat. **209**).

Fig. 583 Termonfechin, Co. Louth. East face of cross. Detail of shaft (Cat. 209).

Fig. 584   Termonfechin, Co. Louth. East face of cross. Detail of shaft and head (Cat. **209**).

Figs. 585-586   Termonfechin, Co. Louth (Cat. 209): 585 South side of cross. – 586 Detail of underside of ring.

Fig. 587 Termonfechin, Co. Louth. West face of cross (Cat. **209**).

Fig. 588   Termonfechin, Co. Louth. North side of cross (Cat. 209).

Figs. 589-590   Tihilly, Co. Offaly (Cat. **210**): 589 East face of cross. – 590 South side.

Figs. 591-592 Tihilly, Co. Offaly (Cat. **210**): 591 West face of cross. – 592 North side.

Fig. 594 Tonaknock, Co. Kerry. West face of cross (Cat. 211).

Fig. 593 Tihilly, Co. Offaly. Capstone of cross, now in University College, Dublin (Cat. 210).

Fig. 597 Tory Island, Co. Donegal. Fragment of a (?)cross-shaft (Cat. **214**).

Fig. 596 Tory Island, Co. Donegal. Tower Cross. Fragment of one face (Cat. **213**).

Fig. 595 Tory Island, Co. Donegal. T-shaped cross. West face (Cat. **212**).

Fig. 598   Toureen Peakaun, Co. Tipperary. East face of shaft, with arm-fragment on the left (Cat. **215**).

Fig. 599   Toureen Peakaun, Co. Tipperary. West face of shaft (Cat. **215**).

Figs. 600-601 Tuam, Co. Galway. Market Cross (Cat. **216/217**): 600 East side. – 601 Detail of shaft.

Figs. 602-603   Tuam, Co. Galway. Market Cross (Cat. **216**): 602 East side. Detail of base. – 603 South face. Detail of base.

Figs. 604-605   Tuam, Co Galway. Market Cross (Cat. **216/217**): 604 South face. – 605 Detail of shaft.

Figs. 606-607   Tuam, Co. Galway. Market Cross (Cat. **216**):   606 West side. Detail of base. – 607 North face. Detail of base.

Figs. 608-609   Tuam, Co. Galway. Market Cross (Cat. **216/217**): 608 West side. – 609 Detail of shaft.

Figs. 610-611   Tuam, Co. Galway. Market Cross (Cat. **216/217**): 610 North face. – 611 Detail of shaft.

Fig. 612 Tuam, Co. Galway. Market Cross. South face. Detail of head (Cat. 217).

Fig. 613 Tuam, Co. Galway. Market Cross. North face. Detail of head (Cat. **217**).

Figs. 614-615 Tuam, Co. Galway. Cross-shaft in Cathedral (Cat. **218**): 614 East face. – 615 South side.

Figs. 616-617   Tuam, Co. Galway. Cross-shaft in Cathedral (Cat. **218**): 616 West face, *c.* 1930.
617 North side.

Fig. 618 Tuam, Co. Galway. Cross-head from St. John's Abbey, now in storage (Cat. **219**).

Fig. 619   Tullaghan, Co. Leitrim. South face of cross (Cat. **220**).

Fig. 620   Tullaghore, Co. Antrim. West face of cross (Cat. **221**).

Figs. 621-622 Tullow, Co. Carlow. Cross-head (Cat. **222**): 621 East face. – 622 West face.

Fig. 623   Tullow, Co. Carlow. Cross-head. North side (Cat. **222**).

Fig. 624   Tully, Co. Dublin. West face of cross (Cat. **223**).

Figs. 625-626 Tybroughney, Co. Kilkenny. Pillar (Cat. **224**): 625 East face. – 626 South side.

Figs. 627–628   Tybroughney, Co. Kilkenny. Pillar (Cat. **224**):   627 West face. – 628 North side.

Fig. 629   Tynan, Co. Armagh. Island Cross. East face (Cat. **225**).

Fig. 630   Tynan, Co. Armagh. Island Cross. West face (Cat. **225**).

Figs. 631-632   Tynan, Co. Armagh. Terrace Cross (Cat. **226**): 631 East face. – 632 South side. Shaft.

Figs. 633-634   Tynan, Co. Armagh. Terrace Cross (Cat. **226**): 633 West face. – 634 North side.

Figs. 635-636   Tynan, Co. Armagh. Village Cross (Cat. **227/228**): 635 East face. – 636 North side.

Fig. 637   Tynan, Co. Armagh. Village Cross. West face (Cat. **227/228**).

Fig. 638   Tynan, Co. Armagh. Well
Cross. North side (Cat. **229**).

Fig. 639   Tynan, Co. Armagh. Well Cross. East face (Cat. **229**).

Fig. 640   Tynan, Co. Armagh. Well Cross. West face (Cat. **229**).

Fig. 642 Ullard, Co. Kilkenny. East face of cross. Head (Cat. **231**).

Fig. 641 Tynan, Co. Armagh. Fragment of a ring of a cross on a wall (Cat. **230**).

Figs. 643-644 Ullard, Co. Kilkenny (Cat. **231**): 643 East face of cross. Base and part of shaft. – 644 West face. Head.

Fig. 645   Waterstown, Co. Carlow. North face of cross (Cat. **232**).

Figs. 646-647 Provenance uncertain (Donaghmore, Co Meath?). Cross-fragment in the National Museum (Cat. **233**): 646 Face 1. – 647 Face 2.